I0814250

MODERN STARS

CAITLIN CLARK

by Megan Clendenan

Essential Library
An Imprint of Abdo Publishing
abdobooks.com

ABDOBOOKS.COM

Published by Abdo Publishing, a division of ABDO, PO Box 398166, Minneapolis, Minnesota 55439.

Printed in the United States of America, North Mankato, Minnesota.
102025
012026

Cover Photo: Dylan Buell/Getty Images Sport/Getty Images
Interior Photos: Steven King/Icon Sportswire/Getty Images, 5, 6; Serhii Chrucky/Alamy, 9; Melissa Tamez/Icon Sportswire/Getty Images, 13; Mihai Andritoiu/Shutterstock Images, 15; Gregory Shamus/Getty Images Sport/Getty Images, 17; Shutterstock Images, 19, 38; Hannah Foslien/Getty Images Sport/Getty Images, 21; Luke Lu/Diamond Images/Getty Images, 25; Sergey Kolesnikov/Shutterstock Images, 26; Marc Piscotty/Icon Sportswire/Getty Images, 32; Tami Ruble/Alamy, 35; Matthew Holst/Getty Images Sport/Getty Images, 41, 63; G. Fiume/Getty Images Sport/Getty Images, 43; Charlie Neibergall/AP Images, 44; Scott Stuart/ZUMA Press, Inc./Alamy, 46; David Berding/Getty Images Sport/Getty Images, 49; Caean Couto/AP Images, 54; Tom Pennington/Getty Images Sport/Getty Images, 55; Ron Jenkins/Getty Images Sport/Getty Images, 57; Tony Gutierrez/AP Images, 58; Greg Fiume/NCAA Photos/Getty Images, 65; Steph Chambers/Getty Images Sport/Getty Images, 66; Sarah Stier/Getty Images Sport/Getty Images, 69, 72; John Nacion/Sportico/Getty Images, 71; Elsa/Getty Images Sport/Getty Images, 75; Greg Fiume/Getty Images Sport/Getty Images, 77, 89; Jeffrey Brown/Icon Sportswire/Getty Images, 79; Brian Spurlock/Icon Sportswire/Getty Images, 80; Joe Buglewicz/Getty Images Sport/Getty Images, 86; Ron Hoskins/NBAE/National Basketball Association/Getty Images, 87; Michael Reaves/Getty Images Sport/Getty Images, 90; Dylan Buell/Getty Images Sport/Getty Images, 93; Jamie Squire/Getty Images Sport/Getty Images, 97; Jasey Michelle Bradwell/NBAE/National Basketball Association/Getty Images, 98

Editor: Riley Madsen
Series Designer: Karli Hughes

Library of Congress Control Number: 2025939319

PUBLISHER'S CATALOGING-IN-PUBLICATION DATA

Names: Clendenan, Megan, author.
Title: Caitlin Clark / by Megan Clendenan
Description: Minneapolis, Minnesota: Abdo Publishing, 2026 | Series: Modern stars | Includes online resources and index.
Identifiers: ISBN 9781098298098 (lib. bdg.) | ISBN 9798384931898 (ebook)
Subjects: LCSH: Clark, Caitlin, 2002- --Juvenile literature. | Women basketball players--United States--Biography--Juvenile literature. | Female athletes--Biography--Juvenile literature. | Indiana Fever (Basketball team)--Juvenile literature. | Guards (Basketball) --Juvenile literature.
Classification: DDC 796.323--dc23

CONTENTS

CHAPTER ONE

THE TIPPING POINT

On February 6, 2022, 20-year-old Caitlin Clark, a sophomore at the University of Iowa, stepped into the Crisler Center in Ann Arbor, Michigan. Fans had gathered to watch her team, the Hawkeyes, play the University of Michigan Wolverines. She anticipated a tough game.

The Hawkeyes were ranked number 21 among women's college basketball teams, and the Wolverines were ranked number six. And the Hawkeyes were missing two of their best players. Clark, known for her competitive spirit, was determined to lead her team to victory despite it all.

Players, fans, and cheerleaders displayed pink during a 2022 Michigan–Iowa game. >>

MICHIG
IOWA
22

Clark sank six three-pointers during the game against Michigan.

Clark and the Hawkeyes marched onto the court wearing pink uniforms to raise awareness for breast cancer research. Clark honored Dan Keough, a family friend who had battled cancer, by wearing his last name on her shirt. The teams faced off for the jump ball, and it was game on. Her shoes squeaking, Clark quickly dribbled down the court and scored the first basket for Iowa.

However, after two and a half minutes, Michigan had a 7–2 lead. By halftime, Iowa trailed 48–36, and the pressure on Clark and her teammates swelled. They showed impressive hustle, shooting, passing, and dribbling against Michigan's tough defense, but at the end of the third quarter, Michigan led 70–54.

As the fourth quarter started, Clark realized that if the Hawkeyes were going to make a comeback, it had to start now. Her thousands of hours of practice had prepared her for this moment, and she refused to give up. With 4:50 remaining in the fourth quarter, Clark dodged defenders, found an opening, and took a deep three-point shot. The ball swished through the net.

But the Hawkeyes needed more. With only 3:12 remaining, Clark nailed another bold three-point shot. With each successful shot Clark netted, the pressure on Michigan increased. The Hawkeyes were closing in. With 2:32 left, Clark made another three-point shot, yet Iowa still lagged behind 87–78. With defenders shadowing her every move, Clark barreled up the court and strategically stopped just outside the three-point line. With 1:39 left, she made yet another three-pointer.

Clark's performance had altered the game's atmosphere and energized her team. Michigan fans anxiously checked the clock. But when the buzzer sounded, the Hawkeyes hadn't been able to take the lead despite Clark heroically scoring 17 points in under four minutes. Michigan held on to win 98–90. Even so, Clark was undoubtedly the star of the game, scoring 46 points—her best college performance to date.

IN THE SPOTLIGHT

The next day, Clark was a viral star on social media. Basketball fans were buzzing about her performance. Even people who typically didn't follow basketball were talking about Clark. Some of her risky three-point shots taken from near midcourt sparked criticism online, but she also received plenty of support, including a post from National Basketball Association (NBA) star Trae Young, who wrote, "Can't say nothing when it goes in. She's tough."[1] YouTube star MrBeast, who had millions of followers, also posted about Clark, promising to watch future games.

A few weeks later, on February 27, 2022, Iowa was up against Michigan again, but this time the stakes were higher. If the Hawkeyes won, they would secure the Big Ten regular-season title. In the locker room before the game, Clark glanced at her goals written on a paper in her locker: "Vision: Big Ten Champions. Final Four." These words inspired her

BIG TEN TOURNAMENT

The Big Ten Women's Basketball Tournament is a competition held each year in early March at the end of the regular season. The winner secures an automatic spot in the NCAA Tournament later in March. In 2023, Clark and the Hawkeyes reached the championship game. Attendance for the tournament was 47,923. The next year, with Clark and the Hawkeyes participating again, the Big Ten Women's Basketball Tournament sold out for the first time, attracting more than 109,000 fans.[2]

Carver–Hawkeye Arena is named after Roy J. Carver, a businessman who donated $2 million toward the construction of the arena.

as she thought, "We're here. This is our moment. Let's go take it."[3]

Clark walked through the tunnel and onto the court with her team amid the electrifying cheers of a packed home crowd at Carver–Hawkeye Arena in Iowa City, Iowa. Turning to her teammate Gabbie Marshall, Clark said that she had the chills. The sold-out crowd buzzed with anticipation, wondering whether Clark would deliver another record-setting performance.

Her first big moment came about halfway through the first quarter when she dribbled up the court, hopped, and launched the ball from almost midcourt, scoring three points. The crowd erupted. But Michigan soon

LOGO THREES

Clark excels at sinking shots from beyond the three-point line. Though only implemented by the NBA in 1979 and the NCAA in 1986, the three-point line changed the game and brought new energy and excitement to basketball. "Logo threes," shots often made by Clark, are called that because they are taken from near the middle of the court where the home team's logo is painted on the floor. This is several feet behind the three-point line. She credits her dad for making sure she developed shooting from an early age.

overtook Iowa, and the Hawkeyes had to focus on defense as Michigan led the rest of the first quarter.

In the second quarter, the atmosphere shifted. With the score tied at 34–34, Clark scored two free throws. Then, she scored another three-pointer from the logo, sending the crowd into a frenzy. She continued to deliver daring three-point shots, and Iowa's score climbed.

With a solid lead, Clark spent the fourth quarter assisting her teammates. "I was just passing [the ball] to them and they were knocking it down. . . . That's Iowa basketball the way we share the ball," she said afterward.[4]

As the buzzer sounded, Iowa won 104–80. Ecstatic fans jumped to their feet, cheering for Clark and the Hawkeyes. Dressed in bright yellow uniforms, the players celebrated their win together at midcourt. Clark had scored 38 points, and the Hawkeyes were cochampions of the Big Ten, sharing the honor with Ohio State University.

RISE TO FAME

While Clark's spectacular sophomore season raised her public profile, this was only one stop on her exceptional journey. Her ability to sink three-point shots would become legendary, drawing comparisons to NBA superstar Steph Curry and inspiring young fans across the nation. Her feisty attitude sometimes put her in the spotlight, but she thrived under pressure and could find openings to shoot even when closely guarded.

Clark's rise to one of the most recognizable young athletes in the United States reached a tipping point during these February 2022 games. In her subsequent college years, women's basketball games began to sell out arenas. This was an exciting trend, as women's college basketball has historically received far less attention than the men's game. Change was underway, and Clark's daring style of basketball played a significant role in this shift.

After Iowa won a share of the Big Ten championship in February 2022, Clark's star continued to rise, both on and off the court. The excitement surrounding Clark's performances had attracted new fans, a phenomenon first labeled by one Iowa writer as the "Caitlin Clark Effect." A writer for the National Collegiate Athletic Association (NCAA) wrote, "Women's basketball has seen a rocketlike

"I came to Iowa with huge aspirations and now I'm getting to play in front of 15,000-plus every single night and that's so cool."[7]

—Caitlin Clark, 2024

rise in popularity in recent years, and Iowa senior Caitlin Clark . . . has provided a lot of the fuel."[5]

In March 2024, Clark, playing in front of a sold-out crowd at Carver–Hawkeye Arena, became the highest scorer in NCAA history, breaking Pete Maravich's record of 3,667 points set in 1970.[6] This achievement solidified Clark's status as a generational player, one who exceeds all expectations and brings significant impact to her teams and her sport. And yet, Clark was just starting her career. On April 15, 2024, she was selected by the Indiana Fever as the first pick in the Women's National Basketball Association (WNBA) Draft.

CLARK AND THE IOWA STARTING FIVE

During Clark's time as a Hawkeye, she was one of five regular starters, along with Kate Martin, Monika Czinano, McKenna Warnock, and Gabbie Marshall. Over the years, these players formed a close-knit group. At first, however, the other four had to adjust and stand their ground when faced with Clark's competitive nature. They learned to deal with her moments of frustration and impatience. Through this process, they developed a strong and cohesive team.

Today, Clark is celebrated worldwide for her athleticism. Like many athletes, she started out as a child with big dreams and spent countless hours playing and practicing her skills. From the beginning of her journey, she received support from her family, coaches, and teammates, and with this caring network and Clark's hard work, her dreams came true.

Clark has brought unprecedented attention to the WNBA and the Indiana Fever.

CHAPTER TWO

PLAYING SPORTS WITH THE BOYS

Caitlin Clark was born on January 22, 2002, in Des Moines, Iowa. With two brothers, she is the middle child in her family. She is the only girl born to Brent Clark, a sales executive, and Anne Nizzi-Clark, a marketing professional.

Her father played college basketball and baseball. Caitlin's mother is the daughter of Bob Nizzi, a high school football coach and counselor who worked for many years at Dowling Catholic, the high school that all the Clark children attended. Caitlin grew up in West Des Moines, where she played sports with her many cousins and her brothers, Blake and Colin.

Des Moines is the most populous city in Iowa. >>

Both of Caitlin's brothers also excelled at sports. Blake became a college football quarterback at Iowa State University, and Colin played high school basketball and participated in track and field. The close-knit family often played and watched sports together. One of Clark's main role models was her older cousin Audrey Faber, who played basketball for Dowling Catholic. After watching Audrey win a state title as a junior, Caitlin dreamed of the day her chance would come.

PARTICIPATING IN SPORTS AS A YOUNG GIRL

Caitlin's parents remember that when she was only two or three years old, her day care staff noticed her impressive motor skills and coordination as well as her competitive nature. Caitlin wanted to win, whether in sports, at school, or even when playing board games such as Candy Land. In first grade, Caitlin raced to complete a math quiz, and her mom remembers Caitlin was focused more on whom she would beat rather than the material itself.

Caitlin remembers feeling competitive in everything when she was younger. "When we trick-or-treated in Des Moines growing up," she recalled, "I would be so sweaty under my costume because I was in a dead sprint from

Caitlin's parents have supported her basketball journey from the beginning.

house to house. I had to have the most candy. That's how I operated."[1]

Caitlin and her brothers played competitively as children and often played basketball in their basement. One time, Caitlin was playing a one-on-one game with Colin. She accidentally pushed him into the corner of a wall. Colin ended up with a large cut on his head that needed four staples to close. Caitlin didn't mean to hurt him. She was just doing everything she could to get the ball and score.

"As a young girl I was super competitive. . . . Any sport I was doing, but especially in basketball, I always wanted to be the best, and there [were] times where I definitely wasn't. . . . You get back up and you keep trying."[3]

—Caitlin Clark, March 2024

Even though Blake was older, stronger, and faster, Caitlin wanted to play with him and his friends. She had to find a way to hold her own, even when it was difficult. Caitlin appreciated this challenge, as it helped her develop her basketball skills.

JOINING THE BOYS' LEAGUE

At the age of five, Caitlin was already making baskets on a six-foot (1.8 m) hoop, sometimes from 15 feet (4.6 m) away. "I don't recall that she would ever miss a shot," her father, Brent, said. "She would just pull up from [the] free throw line and swish."[2] Caitlin's parents enrolled her in a boys' basketball league since there wasn't a girls' league available for her age group. In the boys' league, she quickly learned to hold her own against bigger players.

During one game, Caitlin was being pushed around by a larger boy on the court and began to cry out of frustration. Brent, who was helping coach the team, benched her and told her she could continue playing once she had calmed down. After a few minutes, Caitlin

Some youth leagues in basketball and other sports are mixed gender.

returned to the game with a new strategy. She went right at the boy and knocked him out of bounds.

Caitlin continued to play in boys' leagues. When she was in second grade, after her team won a game, another parent complained to the league that a girl shouldn't be playing with the boys. The complaint did not push Caitlin out, and she was named the league's most valuable player (MVP) that season.

Caitlin's performance on the soccer field was similarly impressive. She played in a league with both boys and girls, demonstrating leadership even at her young age. Russ Trimble, the mayor of Des Moines, recalls his son playing youth soccer with Caitlin. He says, "She was all over the place . . . telling them where to go, what to do. . . . She was probably the most intense player on that field."[4]

Caitlin continued to play in predominantly boys' basketball and soccer leagues until around sixth grade. Her parents wanted her to play with similarly competitive kids because that's what Caitlin wanted. She felt challenged but confident. She remembers her attitude at the time: being a girl doesn't hold her back from doing anything.

DREAMS FOR THE FUTURE

Caitlin relished competition and had big dreams for her future. In second grade, she wrote a list of her life goals, with her top one being to play in the WNBA. But her competitive spirit sometimes made things difficult. She struggled with losing, her emotions sometimes getting the better of her and causing her to burst into tears. But even when she became frustrated in defeat, she persevered.

When Caitlin was ten, she and her dad traveled to Minneapolis, Minnesota, to attend a WNBA game. There, Caitlin saw Maya Moore of the Minnesota Lynx play. After the game, when Moore was speaking and the fans were allowed on the court, Caitlin ran over and hugged her. After the game, Caitlin begged her father to add a three-point line to their driveway basketball court.

He agreed, tearing up grass and pouring concrete to extend the playing area.

FINDING HER SPORT

Besides basketball and soccer, Caitlin also played volleyball, softball, and tennis. She also briefly tried piano lessons. In softball, her skills were good enough to play two age levels higher. Even so, Caitlin found the pace of softball too slow, and at times she became frustrated when other players had a hard time catching her throws.

Caitlin stopped playing softball in fifth grade, but she continued with soccer, tennis, and basketball. Fiercely competitive, she developed her skills by practicing tennis against the garage wall and shooting hoops with her dad. Brent encouraged her to shoot the ball from all distances, so she put in the work on

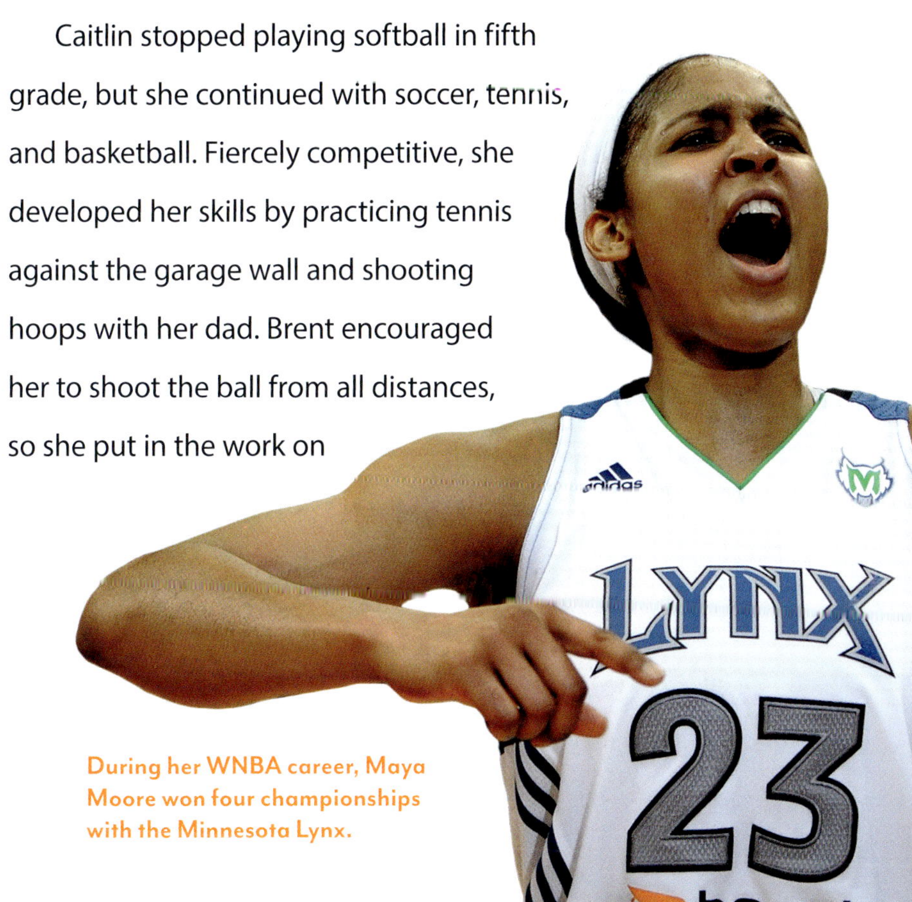

During her WNBA career, Maya Moore won four championships with the Minnesota Lynx.

her three-point shooting. They spent many enjoyable hours together, and when it was time to go inside, Caitlin learned by watching NBA stars such as LeBron James and Kevin Durant on TV.

MEETING MAYA MOORE

Maya Moore, one of the biggest stars in the WNBA, played for the Minnesota Lynx during Caitlin's childhood. Moore had been the number one pick in the 2011 WNBA Draft and went on to lead the Lynx to four titles. Caitlin considers the first time she met Moore to be a life-changing moment, and it drives her to always make time for young fans who approach her for autographs.

In sixth grade Caitlin joined the All-Iowa Attack, a high-level travel basketball program. The All-Iowa Attack allowed Caitlin to play competitively with girls for the first time. Caitlin's talent and work ethic were quickly noticed by Dickson Jensen, the program director. Soon Caitlin was playing several grade levels above her own so that she would be challenged by players of similar skill.

RECRUITERS TAKE NOTICE

When Caitlin was in sixth grade, Iowa assistant coach and recruiter Jan Jensen heard about her talent and went to Des Moines to watch her play. Jensen observed a confident player making challenging passes and already sinking the kind of deep three-point shots that would later make her famous. But because Caitlin was only in sixth grade, Jensen could not approach her directly to recruit her for college.

Aside from the All-Iowa Attack team, Caitlin's middle school coaches asked her to play for both the seventh-grade and eighth-grade teams. However, her parents were concerned about her losing the love of the game, and Caitlin recalls her mom insisting that she not play more than two or three games a day.

At that time, Caitlin wanted to play as much as possible. But looking back, she appreciated the boundaries her parents set. By eighth grade, Caitlin was playing with and against high school seniors, and her talents were beginning to gain wider recognition.

PLAYING MULTIPLE SPORTS

Building a strong foundation of athletic skills by playing in a variety of sports is the best way to eventually excel at an elite level. Young athletes who play multiple sports learn a range of transferable skills. A 2016 study found that high school athletes who focus on only one sport are more likely to suffer from injuries. Caitlin credits her experience playing numerous sports with helping her excel in her basketball career.

CHAPTER THREE

DEVELOPING SKILLS AND STYLE

In the fall of 2016, Caitlin started high school. She attended Dowling Catholic High School in Des Moines, a private faith-based high school that her older brother, Blake, also attended. Going to Dowling Catholic was part of family tradition. Caitlin's mother and aunts had also attended the school.

Caitlin joined the basketball team at Dowling Catholic while still playing on the All-Iowa Attack team. Her high school coach, Kristin Meyer, immediately noticed Caitlin's talent. In fact, Meyer had seen Caitlin play the previous year, and Caitlin's skills, vision, and shooting abilities were obvious to her. Caitlin dedicated herself to her training in the gym and on

Caitlin played for the All-Iowa Attack until she graduated from high school. >>

ATTACK
22
GIRLS EYBL

Playing multiple sports can reduce an athlete's chances of overuse injuries and improve their motor skills.

the court. She loved to experiment with difficult passes and take shots from various angles and distances. While she dreamed of playing in the WNBA, Caitlin rarely spoke of these aspirations. Instead, she focused on the present and dedicated her time and attention to building her skills.

Caitlin's perseverance was key to her later success, but first she needed to make a name for herself at Dowling Catholic. During her freshman season, Caitlin averaged 15.3 points and 4.7 assists per game, and she helped lead the team to the state quarterfinals. She was named to the all-state team, an impressive achievement for a freshman.

A BUSY SPORTS SCHEDULE

Basketball wasn't Caitlin's only sport that year. When tryouts for the soccer team were held in March 2017, she showed up ready and enthusiastic. Joining the team as a forward, she quickly demonstrated her ability to score and make quick decisions under pressure. Caitlin's powerful shots, physical strength, and ability to read the game made her a standout player.

Playing both basketball and soccer kept Caitlin busy. Often she had to choose between them. She missed

BURNOUT

Playing competitive sports is physically and mentally demanding. Talented, hardworking high school athletes risk burnout due to stress from injuries, intense training, fear of failure, and the pressure to excel. Burnout is one of the main reasons athletes quit sports in high school. However, research shows that strong family support like the kind Caitlin received from her parents can significantly decrease the risk of burnout.

some soccer games due to basketball commitments, playing in only six soccer games during her freshman year. But she made the most of those six games, scoring 26 goals.[1] She was the only freshman named to the all-state team.

Despite her skill in soccer, Caitlin's heart was in basketball. She decided to leave soccer to focus on basketball after her sophomore year. But she credits soccer with helping her improve her basketball game by teaching her how to understand angles and to anticipate open space on the court to make and receive passes.

INVITATION TO TEAM USA

In March 2017, Caitlin received an exciting letter—an invitation from USA Basketball to try out for the Team USA Under-16 girls' basketball team. There were only 12 spots available, and if Caitlin earned one of them, she would have the opportunity to compete in a tournament in Buenos Aires, Argentina, in the summer of 2017. Caitlin began to prepare.

Since the international three-point line is farther back, Caitlin's coach marked the gym floor with black tape at that distance for Caitlin to practice her shots. The grueling six-day tryouts would take place in high-altitude Boulder,

Colorado, so Caitlin trained using a special mask to help adapt her breathing.

TRAINING AT HIGH ALTITUDE

Competing at high-altitude locations, such as Boulder, Colorado, can pose challenges for athletes who live at a lower altitude, such as Des Moines, Iowa, where Caitlin lived. There is less pressure in the atmosphere at high altitude, making less oxygen available in each breath. Athletes must work harder at altitude to get the same amount of oxygen to their muscles.

With each round of the selection process, the pressure increased, both mentally and physically. During the last round, when the coaches would choose the final 12 from the remaining 18 players, they met with each girl individually. Caitlin sat nervously through the meeting. When she received the news that she had made the team, she was excited and relieved. "It's a big honor. . . . It hasn't quite sunk in," Caitlin said afterward.[2]

The team trained at the United States Olympic Training Center and then traveled to Buenos Aires in June 2017 for the tournament. In the team's first game, Caitlin scored 11 points to help the team win 91–33 over Colombia. Proudly wearing her Team USA jersey, Caitlin helped the USA Under-16 team win the gold medal.

However, the following year did not go as Caitlin had hoped. In May 2018, she tried out for the Team USA

Under-17 team. She felt confident about her chances considering her strong performance the previous year. However, this time Caitlin did not make the cut. Meyer, her coach at Dowling Catholic, recalled that she played well, but there were many other talented players for the committee to consider. Clark returned home to Des Moines motivated by the experience and determined to train even harder.

MANAGING FRUSTRATION

Years of practicing the fundamentals of basketball with her dad in her driveway were now paying off. Caitlin had excellent control while dribbling, passing, and shooting. She understood the game, anticipating passing opportunities and finding open spaces to shoot with remarkable accuracy.

But at the same time, Caitlin had her struggles. Areas of her game needed improvement. Whatever Caitlin was attempting, whether that was a basketball shot, a school project or test, or even a yoga move, she always wanted it to be perfect. Her competitive nature led to frustration with teammates who missed her passes.

Managing her emotions and high expectations was difficult. She could be impatient, expressing her frustration through negative body language such as stomping her feet or throwing her arms up.

Meyer recognized that Caitlin's competitive nature and advanced basketball skills were causing difficulties with her teammates. Meyer took video footage of Caitlin's negative body language and used it as a teaching tool to help Caitlin understand how her actions appeared to others. Meyer urged her to not dwell on any one play but instead focus on the next one.

DEALING WITH PRESSURE

Throughout her high school years, Caitlin was in high demand as a player. Playing for Dowling Catholic, Caitlin thrived on pressure and consistently rose to the occasion. In her junior season, Caitlin averaged 32.6 points, 6.8 rebounds, and 3.6 assists per game.[3] In one game

STRUGGLING WITH PERFECTIONISM

Caitlin holds herself to high standards and has acknowledged her struggles with perfectionism. Perfectionism is different than the desire to excel. It can involve unrealistic expectations for oneself and others. When these expectations aren't achieved, it can negatively affect mental health, happiness, and relationships with friends or teammates. Coach Meyer helped Caitlin reframe her expectations, seek support, and practice self-compassion, all strategies to manage perfectionism.

Caitlin's high school basketball career had made her a rising star.

at Mason City High School, she scored 60 points, even though Mason City focused its defense on her.

Caitlin made three-point shots from several feet behind the line, an uncommon feat for a high school junior. Dowling Catholic won 90–78. Afterward, Mason City students lined up to get her autograph.

Facing occasional chants of "Overrated! Overrated!" from opposing fans, Caitlin stayed focused, finding that the pressure motivated her to excel. "The bigger the crowd, the louder the crowd—she loves it," Meyer said.[4] Caitlin's reputation grew, and she was named the 2018–19 Gatorade Iowa Girls' Basketball Player of the Year. This prestigious award recognizes athletic and academic excellence. As Caitlin prepared to enter her final year of high school, she faced an important decision—where to attend college.

CHAPTER FOUR

COLLEGE RECRUITMENT

Caitlin was being recruited for college even before high school. Caitlin's father remembers college coaches watching Caitlin's All-Iowa Attack games from the bleachers. After she received a recruitment letter during the summer before seventh grade, her parents asked her brother Blake to get the mail so that Caitlin wouldn't see any others. They wanted her to enjoy middle school, spend time with friends, and not worry about college recruitment.

By the summer before her freshman year of high school, recruiters were calling Meyer, the coach at Dowling Catholic. Meyer already knew that Caitlin was an exceptionally talented player, but it became

College recruiters and scouts sometimes attend high school sports games and tournaments to spot talented athletes. >>

LAKEWOOD PARK
PANTHERS
PANTHERS
21

increasingly evident when, before Caitlin had played a single high school game, Meyer received a call from a Division I college coach in Texas who was interested in recruiting Caitlin. Meyer received calls from recruiters nationwide during Caitlin's freshman and sophomore years.

Mail from college programs began to pile up. Caitlin's parents were adamant that she would have a typical high school experience, and so they did their best to shield her from the recruitment process. Caitlin appreciated her parents' support because she didn't want the recruitment process to overwhelm her, and thanks to her coach and family, it didn't.

WHY UCONN NEVER SHOWED INTEREST

Even as offers arrived from colleges across the country, the University of Connecticut did not show interest. UConn coach Geno Auriemma had already recruited Paige Bueckers, who is a point guard like Caitlin, and so he didn't need another player for that role. Additionally, he believed Caitlin's negative body language on the court would not have been a good fit for the team.

Recruiters frequently came to watch Caitlin practice, and at one home game, about a dozen coaches sat in the bleachers watching her play. One school that Caitlin had hoped would recruit her was the University of Connecticut, the school her WNBA role model,

Maya Moore, had attended. However, to Caitlin's disappointment, UConn showed no interest.

Despite all this attention, Caitlin wanted to be treated like everyone else. She continued to work hard not only at basketball but also in school, taking advanced geometry and advanced chemistry as a sophomore and achieving a 3.82 GPA that year. Friendly and sociable, Caitlin was considered the go-to ambassador for potential Dowling Catholic students who wanted a tour of the school.

KEEPING HER OPTIONS OPEN

Later in high school, Caitlin and her family visited colleges around the country. They traveled to Oregon to visit the University of Oregon and Oregon State University; to Gainesville, Florida, to visit the University of Florida; and to the University of Texas at Austin. Her parents encouraged her to explore schools beyond the Midwest.

The visits gave Caitlin perspective on what it would be like to move away for school and raised questions about life beyond basketball. She considered each school's campus and academic program, the college culture, and how far away from home she might want to live. She needed to figure out whether she wanted to be able to drive home for a weekend.

The University of Iowa is located in Iowa City, in the eastern part of the state.

Although she kept her options open, Caitlin was very interested in the University of Iowa, only a few hours' drive from her home in Des Moines. The school's recruiters had invested significant energy trying to attract Caitlin to their program. Iowa coaches even flew to Bangkok, Thailand, to watch Caitlin play with the Team USA Under-19 team in 2019.

"We knew she was the special one," Iowa associate head coach Jan Jensen said. "Everyone was going to be coming to our state and wanting her. . . . We always understood that it was a marathon."[1]

Still, Caitlin felt that Iowa had been respectful and did not contact her too much. Other colleges overwhelmed her with excessive communication and pressure. "Some schools weed themselves out," Caitlin recalled. "You find schools that are a better fit, more like you."[2]

While considering her choices, Caitlin visited Iowa several times, and she loved the genuine people she met.

One day, she sat in the stands with Iowa star Kathleen Doyle, who was injured at the time and only able to watch practices. "It was great to get her perspective on everything and talk to her and see what she likes," Caitlin said later.[3]

Caitlin didn't rush her decision. Her goal was to decide during her senior year of high school. It was flattering and exciting that many top-tier colleges were pursuing her.

For Caitlin, key considerations included whether she could play right away and contribute to the team, the distance from her home in Iowa, and the coaching style. Caitlin found the Iowa coaches to be down-to-earth, which matched her personality. She also valued how they developed players and their overall approach to the game, a style that she believed would suit her well.

After years of letters, phone calls, and visits from coaches, Caitlin narrowed her choices to Iowa State, the

RECRUITING CAITLIN IN THAILAND

When Caitlin played in Thailand with the Under-19 team, Iowa coaches Lisa Bluder and Jan Jensen went there to show their interest in recruiting her. They flew to see her, but according to NCAA rules, they weren't allowed to speak with her or give her any messages. They could only sit in the stands and hope she noticed them.

University of Iowa, and Notre Dame, in Indiana. All these schools were in the Midwest, something Caitlin deemed important, as she wanted to remain close to her family.

Her family hoped she would attend Notre Dame. The University of Notre Dame is a Catholic institution, though it welcomes students of all faiths. Caitlin's family is Catholic: she attended a Catholic high school and attended church. Notre Dame is also famous for sports.

The school has a long history and a strong reputation for producing champions, including in women's basketball, at the highest level of NCAA athletics. Meyer recalled that Caitlin remained composed during most recruitment visits, with the exception of when Notre Dame coach Muffet McGraw came to observe her play. Caitlin knew that her family was hoping she would choose Notre Dame.

As a child, Caitlin had wanted to attend Notre Dame. "It's the coolest thing in the world," she reflected later. "It has that tradition

THE RIGHT TIME

One important consideration for Caitlin as she chose a college was whether she could make an immediate impact on the basketball court. She considered team dynamics and who was currently playing her position of point guard. At the University of Iowa, star point guard Kathleen Doyle was graduating. This created an opportunity for Caitlin to step into the position right away as a starter.

and they've had so many great players."[4] Notre Dame seemed to meet all Caitlin's requirements, so she called McGraw to say she would join her team.

However, Caitlin wasn't completely convinced of her decision. She still felt Notre Dame might not be the best fit for her. Deep down, she wanted to attend the University of Iowa. Before announcing her decision, she called McGraw to explain she had changed her mind. McGraw was understanding.

Caitlin then called a family meeting to let her parents know she would be attending Iowa. Her parents listened to her reasons and respected her choice. Iowa coach Lisa Bluder was thrilled. Caitlin was rated as the number four prospect in the country in women's basketball, and her commitment was a big win for Iowa. Caitlin had big dreams for the Hawkeyes. The team hadn't reached the Final Four of the NCAA Tournament since 1993, and Caitlin was determined to lead it to a championship.

Lisa Bluder became the Iowa women's basketball head coach in 2000.

CHAPTER FIVE

NUMBER 22 IOWA

In the fall of 2020, Clark moved to Iowa City to begin her freshman year at the University of Iowa. However, this year would be unlike any other, as the world was still adjusting to the COVID-19 pandemic, caused by the rapid spread of the SARS-CoV-2 virus in early 2020. The pandemic resulted in many restrictions on public life in order to reduce the spread of the virus. Games were attended by few or no fans. Tournaments were canceled.

Clark also faced many new challenges. She was living away from her family for the first time. She had to choose college courses. And she had to build relationships with new coaches and teammates.

Clark's jersey number references her birthday, January 22. >>

CLARK
22

Starting her freshman year, Clark built tight bonds with several of her Iowa teammates.

Clark took various courses before ultimately deciding to major in marketing. She was drawn to the major after hearing success stories from former students. It would prove to be an excellent decision, as opportunities for college athletes to promote themselves opened up during her time at Iowa.

Clark realized early in college that the players would be more competitive and skilled. This meant she needed to ensure she was as fast and strong as possible. She started spending more time in the weight room.

Clark also adjusted to the responsibilities of living independently. She later recalled an incident during her freshman year when she and teammate Kate Martin both slept in past the time they needed to get on the bus after an away game. They woke up to their phones ringing and someone knocking on the door and realized instantly they were late.

FRESHMAN SEASON AS A HAWKEYE

Many of Clark's teammates reached out to her before she even arrived on campus. In her first game as a Hawkeye, she scored 27 points, including three three-point shots. "I set my goals pretty high," she said after the game. "It's a good start to the season for sure."[1] Her teammates recognized Clark's talent and sensed that she was exactly what the team needed after Doyle had graduated.

By her fourth game as a Hawkeye, Clark was making a name for herself, scoring a crucial three-point shot from deep to win against Iowa State. However, Clark's competitive nature also caused tension as she adjusted to her new team and they adjusted to her.

Even though Clark had exceptional athletic talent and a deep understanding of the game, coaching her wasn't straightforward. Her competitive spirit and intense emotions could sometimes work against her. In practices and games, she occasionally refused to pass to an open teammate if Clark doubted she would catch the ball. Her teammates struggled to cope with her emotional intensity and frustration when they didn't meet her

Sometimes Clark argued with referees during Iowa games.

high expectations. Teammate Monika Czinano later reflected, "It was apparent that she was going to need to trust us. . . . That takes time when you're a child prodigy."[2]

Throughout Clark's freshman season, Bluder and Jensen worked to find the best approach to coaching her. They learned when to address her negative behavior. This could include throwing her arms up in frustration, stomping her feet at a teammate, or yelling at a referee when she didn't like a call.

Her coaches also learned when to let things slide to preserve her competitive spirit. They felt a responsibility to give her some freedom because of her exceptional talent. However, sometimes teammates felt Clark was being given special treatment.

As Clark's high school coach had done, Bluder and Jensen sat down with Clark and showed her footage of her body language. They wanted to help her understand how this might affect her teammates, and Clark admitted that managing her emotions was a significant challenge. During her freshman season, Clark made progress, learning that when she interacted with teammates in a more positive manner, it elevated everyone's game. The Hawkeyes began to play more cohesively.

NEW OPPORTUNITIES

With Clark on the team, Iowa reached the Sweet Sixteen of the 2021 NCAA Tournament, an exciting milestone. They ultimately lost to UConn 92–72. Nevertheless, Clark's talent had caught further attention. Clark won 13 of the 16 Big Ten Freshman of the Week awards that season and was named the conference's Freshman of the Year.[3]

On July 1, 2021, changes in NCAA rules allowed college athletes to use their name, image, and likeness (NIL) to earn money. This change opened the door for athletes such as Clark to make endorsement deals. Listed as No. 16 on ESPN's 25 Most Marketable College Basketball Players, men or women, Clark was widely seen as someone who could take advantage of the rule change.[4]

She selected her partnerships thoughtfully, starting with the Vinyl Studio, a woman-owned local business in Des Moines that made T-shirts. Clark collaborated with the business to create custom, limited-availability "Back in Gold" T-shirts bearing her initials and jersey number, 22. Various sponsorship and endorsement opportunities arose in subsequent years, and Clark's marketing classes proved valuable even before graduation.

TEAM USA UNDER-19 IN HUNGARY

In the summer before her sophomore year, Clark traveled to Hungary to compete for Team USA in the U-19 World Cup. The team won all seven of its games and secured the gold medal for the USA, and Clark was named tournament MVP. She returned to Iowa ready to implement new defensive strategies for her sophomore season with the Hawkeyes.

After just one year at Iowa, Clark's growing fame had people wondering whether she would transfer schools. However, she wanted to stay. She loved her team, and she liked being close to her family. Her goal was to lead the Hawkeyes to the Final Four of the NCAA Tournament, and she looked forward to making her sophomore year even better.

SOPHOMORE YEAR

With support of her coaches, Clark continued to get better at recognizing and controlling her emotions. One day, Coach Jensen showed Clark a video she had recorded in which Clark appeared visibly frustrated but managed to control her reactions. For Clark, this was excellent progress. As COVID-19 restrictions began to lift, fans traveled long distances to watch her play. After a freshman season playing in empty gyms, she was thrilled that fans could attend games during her sophomore season.

Clark continued to go viral on social media. Clark had been featured by major media sources, bringing national attention to the Hawkeyes. Yahoo Sports noted in January that Clark had put together two straight 30-point triple-doubles: "She is one of six in the sport to record back-to-back 30-point triple-doubles since 2000: Kobe, LeBron, Russ, Harden, Luka, Clark."[5]

Although she was the one in the spotlight, Clark was quick to point out the team effort behind her. "Obviously, a lot of the attention comes to me, and that's really good for our program,"

Clark was the first player in Big Ten women's history to record back-to-back triple-doubles.

she said, "but I always tell my teammates that I wouldn't be where I am if it wasn't for them."[6]

In March 2022, Clark led the Hawkeyes to both a regular-season title and a Big Ten Tournament championship, where she was named Most Outstanding Player. But the second-seeded Hawkeyes were eliminated in the second round of the NCAA Tournament after a disappointing 64–62 upset loss to Creighton. Creighton's Lauren Jensen, who had transferred from Iowa the year before, made a late three-pointer to capture the win.

This was a stunning loss for Clark and the Hawkeyes, who had felt confident they would continue on to the Sweet Sixteen. However, the surprise defeat served as fuel to motivate Clark and her team for the following year's season. "Our early exit last year will always provide that fire for us," Clark reflected later. "No matter what point we're at in the tournament, we still feel like we have a lot to prove."[7]

JUNIOR YEAR BEGINS

By junior year, the crowds watching her games had grown significantly. As Clark's fame grew, she found community with her teammates, who had become a close-knit group.

Her small circle of trusted people included her family, coaching staff, and teammates.

Playing in the Final Four had always been Clark's dream, something she revealed to Bluder when she was first being recruited. Clark believed this was the year they had to make it happen, especially after their upsetting second-round loss the previous season. With Monika Czinano and McKenna Warnock graduating soon, this would be the final season with the same five starters from the previous two years.

The Hawkeyes suffered back-to-back losses early in the season, and Clark continued to struggle with controlling her emotions. She was still prone to outbursts of negativity. But she also displayed moments of self-regulation and growth, choosing to walk off the court for a moment when she needed to cool down.

KEEPING SAFE

As Clark gained fame, concerns for her safety increased. She recalled that after a home game in her sophomore year, she was walking alone to her car when two strangers approached her. She felt uneasy as they asked for her signature on merchandise. When her parents learned of the encounter, they decided it was time to increase her security. From then on, Clark always had a security guard.

Clark's coaches encouraged the entire team to communicate openly each week, which helped them bond as they worked toward their goal of the Final Four. Their conversations during these sessions were honest, and Clark's participation and openness to change helped bring the team together in a positive way.

NCAA TOURNAMENT EXPLAINED

Nicknamed March Madness, the NCAA Tournament happens each year from March to early April. Sixty-eight teams participate, and each team is given a ranking called a seed that determines where it will play in the single-elimination tournament structure. In Clark's freshman year, the Hawkeyes reached the Sweet Sixteen, which is the third round when 16 teams remain. In her sophomore year, her team was eliminated in the second round. In her junior year, it reached the Final Four, a prestigious fifth round consisting of the four remaining teams. Iowa won that round to advance to the championship game.

In the final regular-season game, Iowa faced the University of Indiana, which was ranked number two. It was a tense game, but the Hawkeyes managed to pull ahead in the end for an 86–85 win. Clark and the Hawkeyes then won the Big Ten Tournament and advanced to the NCAA Tournament.

Iowa's first opponent was Southeastern Louisiana University, whom the Hawkeyes soundly defeated 95–43. Clark scored 26 points and had 12 assists in the game.

Czinano also put on an outstanding performance, scoring 22 points.

In the next round, Iowa faced off with the University of Georgia Lady Bulldogs. This game was much more competitive. The Lady Bulldogs took an early lead in the first quarter, but Iowa took control at 6:12 with a layup by Czinano to bring the score to 10–8.

The teams traded the lead back and forth through the first three quarters. However, Iowa rallied in the fourth quarter, holding the lead the whole time until the final buzzer locked in the score at 74–66. Clark had scored 22 points and had 12 assists.

Up next were the University of Colorado Buffaloes. This time, Iowa took an early lead and was eight points ahead halfway through the first quarter. Colorado's offense soon found its footing, however, and the team managed to end the half with a one-point lead.

The halftime break reenergized the Hawkeyes, whose explosive offensive performance in the first five minutes of the third quarter forced Colorado to use two time-outs. After that, Iowa held the lead all the way to the end for a final score of 87–77. Clark supplied 31 of her team's points, helping send the Hawkeyes to the tournament's next round.

Iowa's wins set up an Elite Eight game against the University of Louisville. Even though this was Clark's most important game so far, when she stepped onto the court that day, she did not feel nervous. Clark played exceptionally well, scoring 41 points and making 12 assists, leading Iowa to a 97–83 victory.

The Hawkeyes were headed to the Final Four for the first time since 1993. In a joyful postgame interview, Clark divulged she had visualized herself one day wearing Iowa Final Four gear. "When you dream and work really hard a lot of really cool things can happen," she said.[8]

In a national semifinal game, Clark and the Hawkeyes were set to play against the University of South Carolina Gamecocks. The Gamecocks were the defending national champions and came into the game undefeated at 36–0. As the Hawkeyes arrived, they heard the sounds of enthusiastic fans in the stands.

After defeating Louisville, Iowa received a trophy for coming out on top in its region of the tournament.

Clark often celebrated making a three-pointer by raising three fingers.

The game got off to a slow start, with neither team scoring in the first two minutes. Then Clark put the first points on the board with a layup. Iowa kept that lead throughout the first quarter, which ended 22–13. By halftime, though, the Gamecocks managed to bring their scoring deficit to only one point.

The game remained competitive until the end. With one minute left, South Carolina was behind by two points. To buy more time, the Gamecocks began to foul Clark, sending her to the free throw line twice. She downed all four free throws, bringing the score to 77–73 by the final buzzer. Clark had carried her team through the tense game, scoring 41 points, including five three-point shots. The Hawkeyes would play the championship game against Louisiana State University (LSU).

CHAPTER SIX

THE CAITLIN CLARK EFFECT

On April 2, 2023, Clark and the Hawkeyes arrived at American Airlines Center in Dallas, Texas, to play the NCAA Tournament championship game. A record 9.9 million viewers tuned in to watch on ABC.[1] LSU coaches knew that guarding Clark would be challenging, and they expected her to score a significant number of points.

The coaches believed that the key to winning was stopping Czinano. Although Clark scored 30 points and made eight assists, it wasn't enough. The Hawkeyes lost 102–85 to LSU, led by center Angel Reese, another rising star of women's college basketball.

American Airlines Center is the home of the professional sports teams the Dallas Mavericks and the Dallas Stars. >>

2023 WOMEN'S
FINAL FOUR
DALLAS
AMERICAN AIRLINES CENTER
DO NOT ENTER

Clark and Reese, *right*, agreed that trash talk is simply part of women's basketball.

The game was fiercely competitive. Near the end, as it became clear that LSU would win, Reese gestured to Clark. She pointed to her ring finger to indicate where her tournament ring would go.

After the game, a debate started on social media. Many criticized Reese for exhibiting poor sportsmanship, while others argued that this reaction highlighted a racial double standard for Reese, a Black player. Clark had also engaged in trash talk in other games, but she did not receive as much criticism as Reese.

The on-court moments were discussed in the postgame interviews. "All year I was critiqued about who I was," Reese said. "I don't fit in the box that you all want me to be in. I'm too hood. I'm too ghetto. . . . But when other people do it, you all don't say nothing."[2] A few days later, Clark said that she thought Reese was a tremendous player.

She said, "I think everybody knew there was going to be a little trash talk the entire tournament. It's not just me and Angel. I don't think she should be criticized."[3] This incident marked the beginning of what would become a larger conversation about race, gender, and how female athletes are perceived and celebrated.

GOLF, A FAVORITE HOBBY

Clark first tried golf at the age of six and remembers receiving a set of bright pink golf clubs for her birthday one year as a child. She often asked her dad to take her golfing. She loves being outside and appreciates the individual nature of the sport. This makes it different from the other sports she plays.

Now that Iowa's season was over, Clark spent time relaxing on the golf course. In a conversation with *Golf Digest*, she explained that golf clears her mind while also keeping her active. She even said that playing golf taught her lessons about how to take responsibility as an athlete.

"Obviously in basketball I have four other girls on the court with me that I can lean on if I'm not having a good day or shooting well," she said. "If I'm on the golf course, it's all on me. You have to accept that not every day is gonna be great for you. That's helped me by translating that to basketball."[4]

During the 2023 season, after Iowa had won a game against the University of Nebraska, the website Hawkeyes Wire referred to the rising interest in the Iowa women's basketball team as the Caitlin Clark Effect. When Iowa played South Carolina in the 2023 Final Four, television ratings for the game increased by 72 percent compared with 2022.[5]

In the 2019–2020 season before Clark arrived to play for the Hawkeyes, an adult single-game ticket cost $12. Season tickets were $100. Iowa had sold out only three regular-season games in history.

Ticket sales were limited the next two seasons due to COVID-19. By the 2022–2023 season, Clark's junior year, the cost of season tickets had gone up to $125. The next season, adult season tickets cost $195 and they sold out, as did single-game tickets, which were then being resold for an average of $135 for an away game and $180 for a home game.[6]

Clark signed significant NIL contracts with brands such as Gatorade, State Farm, and Nike. Her marketing major was put to use as she attended corporate brand meetings, filmed commercials, and appeared on billboards. Clark quickly became a household name, and interest in women's college basketball surged. Fans were willing to pay more, travel farther, and even stand outside in the cold waiting to buy a ticket to see her play.

When Clark played, arenas opened extra concession stands, restaurants in the area filled up, and nearby hotels sold out for the night. On television, viewership for women's college basketball increased by 60 percent compared with the previous season, and the women's title game surpassed the viewership for the men's game for the first time in history.[7] Sold-out games were filled with fans—especially young girls—holding posters showing their support for Clark and lining up for autographs.

CLARKONOMICS

As Clark's talent and celebrity status grew, more and more people wanted to see her play. Her presence drove increased ticket sales, resulting in sold-out stadiums, increased business for restaurants and hotels, increased merchandise sales, and significantly more media coverage of women's basketball. This influence and corresponding economic value became known as Clarkonomics, a term coined by college basketball analyst Debbie Antonelli.

BREAKING THE NCAA SCORING RECORD

Against the Michigan Wolverines, Clark caught a pass in the backcourt.

She dribbled a couple of times up the left side, and well behind the three-point line, she launched one of her classic logo-threes. She made it, and with that, she broke the all-time women's scoring record, surpassing Kelsey Plum's mark of 3,527 points.[8] Clark finished the game with a career-high 49 points.

Then, two weeks later, when the Hawkeyes played Ohio State on March 3, Clark was expected to break the all-time NCAA Division I scoring record for women and for men. She needed only 18 points to surpass Pete Maravich's record, which he set after three seasons at LSU from 1967 to 1970. Ticket prices rose on the secondary market, and television viewership spiked as spectators hoped to watch the moment live.

By the second quarter, Clark broke the record and became the all-time leading Division I scorer. This time it wasn't with one of her trademark three-point shots. Instead, Clark broke the record with a free throw.

CLARK'S THREE-POINTERS

After Clark worked on her strength and conditioning in her freshman year, her shooting abilities improved even further. Clark became Iowa's and the Big Ten Tournament's all-time leader in scoring and assists as well as becoming the Division I player with the most three-pointers in a single season. She surpassed the previous record set by NBA superstar Steph Curry in the 2007–2008 season.

Clark and her teammates began to celebrate the moment that she broke Maravich's scoring record.

After celebrating briefly, Clark went on to finish the game with 35 points, nine assists and six rebounds, and Iowa won 93–83. In the stands that night to witness Clark's achievement was Moore, Clark's childhood role model. Clark hadn't intentionally set out to break the record. Now that she had, she planned to return her focus to her team and their upcoming games.

QUESTIONS OF FAVORITISM AND RIVALRY

Clark's rising fame brought her not only celebrity status but also massive sponsorship deals worth millions of dollars. While she has been credited with generating significant interest in women's basketball, some suggest there was favoritism in the way Clark was treated compared with Black players such as Reese. The interactions between Clark and Reese during the 2023 championship game sparked a heated debate about how the two players are perceived by the media and the public.

Clark and Reese were labeled as rivals, but Clark disagreed. "We're not best friends, by any means, but we're very respectful of one another," she said. She also questioned why the media didn't focus more on the game itself, saying, "The only thing people cared about was this controversy that was really fabricated."[9]

Clark has repeatedly been called a generational player in the media. However, commentators have compared her to other players such as Reese, who may also qualify as generational talents. These commentators point out that these other players haven't received the same level of attention or endorsements.

A FINAL SHOT AT THE FINAL FOUR

As March Madness approached in early 2024, tensions rose for Clark and the Hawkeyes. This would be her last

Teammates high-fived Clark as she was introduced at the beginning of the third-round game against Colorado.

chance to try to win a national championship. At times, as in previous years, she struggled to manage her emotions, berating herself and losing patience with her teammates. But at other times, she showed growth in her ability to collaborate with them. Clark knew she needed to focus on playing her best in each game rather than looking too far into the future.

In the first round of the NCAA Tournament, Clark did just that. Playing against the College of the Holy Cross, she led Iowa in scoring, earning 27 points and ten assists. The Hawkeyes soundly defeated the Holy Cross Crusaders 91–65.

In the second round, Iowa faced the West Virginia University Mountaineers. Clark continued to dominate, scoring 32 points, half her team's total score, and downing 11 of her 12 free-throw attempts. The 64–54 win

Clark and Kate Martin, *left*, were emotional as they walked off the court following their loss to South Carolina in the championship game.

against the Mountaineers brought the Hawkeyes to the Sweet Sixteen.

The Colorado Buffaloes were the Hawkeyes' next challengers. The Buffaloes were seeded fifth, making them the toughest team on paper that the Hawkeyes had faced in the tournament so far. But a two-pointer by Clark brought Iowa to an early 2–1 lead, and the Buffaloes were never able to claw back control of the game. The Hawkeyes won 89–68, with Clark scoring 29 points.

In the Elite Eight, Clark and the Hawkeyes once again faced Reese and LSU. Clark scored 41 points and 12 assists, sinking nine three-point shots to lead the Hawkeyes to a 94–87 victory. Afterward, Clark and Reese shook hands at the line, acknowledging each other with nothing but respect.

After their Elite Eight win, the Hawkeyes moved on to the Final Four for the second consecutive year. In the semifinal game against the University of Connecticut, Clark and teammate Hannah Stuelke both scored more than 20 points, leading the team to a 71–69 victory and securing the Hawkeyes a spot in the championship game.

In the championship game against South Carolina, Clark scored 18 points in the first quarter alone. Iowa ended the quarter up seven points, 27–20. In the second quarter, though, Clark made only a single three-pointer, giving South Carolina the chance to pull ahead for a three-point lead at halftime.

Clark's low scoring continued in the third quarter, when she scored only four points. In the end, Iowa lost 87–75. But Clark and the Hawkeyes left the court to a standing ovation after Clark's final college game.

During Clark's time at Iowa, women's college basketball gained more attention than ever before. Television viewership reached all-time highs. *Saturday Night Live* aired a sketch the night before the final game focusing on Clark and her team. It was a mock March Madness postgame show, focusing on how the women's NCAA Tournament had attracted record-setting crowds. The sketch emphasized Clark's impressive shooting skills.

CHAPTER SEVEN

JOINING THE WNBA

Because of a shortened freshman season due to COVID-19 restrictions, Clark had the option to return to Iowa to play a fifth season. However, she felt ready for the next chapter of her life. She entered her name into the WNBA Draft, scheduled for April 15, 2024, in New York City.

It was a whirlwind time for Clark, as the NCAA Tournament had recently wrapped up. Then, only a few days before the draft, Clark appeared on *Saturday Night Live*. She playfully joked with the show's Michael Che about his past jokes about women's basketball. She also expressed gratitude for several Black female players, including Lisa Leslie, Sheryl Swoopes, Cynthia

Clark's WNBA Draft outfit was provided by the luxury fashion brand Prada. >>

PRADA

Cooper, Dawn Staley, and Maya Moore, acknowledging that they had built the foundation for her success.

Many believe there is a racial underpinning to Clark's fame. They note that talented Black WNBA players don't receive the same level of attention she does. In an interview with *Time* in 2024, Clark commented that while she had earned her success, she acknowledged the societal advantages of being white.

MAJOR ENDORSEMENT DEALS

In April 2024, Clark signed an eight-year endorsement deal with Nike worth $28 million.[1] She had been collaborating with Nike since 2022 under NCAA NIL rules, but this marked her first significant sponsorship deal as a professional player. Clark grew up watching Nike athletes and was inspired to be a part of the brand and motivate new athletes. In May 2024, Clark announced an endorsement with Wilson that included the release of a Caitlin Clark signature collection of basketballs with laser engravings. Clark is the first athlete since Michael Jordan to sign a signature basketball with Wilson.

THE WNBA DRAFT

As the draft approached, Clark was anticipated to be the number one pick. She arrived at the draft dressed head to toe in clothes that were a stark contrast to her usual basketball attire. She wore a white satin miniskirt and matching shirt layered over a sparkly rhinestone-embroidered crop top, paired with black leather pumps and accessorized with jewelry.

In a predraft interview, Clark was asked what would go through her mind when her name was called. "Just soak it in and enjoy it," she responded. "You only get to do this one time. It's not like we can do this over again."[2] Clark took a seat at a table with her family, who had supported her from the beginning of her journey. Clark felt anxious as she waited for the announcement, a moment she had dreamed of for years.

"I'm just very lucky to be in this moment, and all these opportunities and these things, they're once in a lifetime. . . . This isn't something everybody gets to do."[3]

—Caitlin Clark, April 2024

As the draft began, WNBA Commissioner Cathy Engelbert strode to the podium. "With the first pick in the 2024 WNBA Draft," Engelbert said, "the Indiana Fever select Caitlin Clark, University of Iowa." As Clark walked to the stage and held up the Fever jersey, the crowd erupted.

Clark later recalled, "[It] definitely shows that the hard work pays off, and I think more than anything . . . I earned

Cathy Engelbert was announced as the new WNBA commissioner on May 15, 2019.

Engelbert presented Clark with a special number one Fever jersey after Clark was drafted.

this moment."[4] She was excited to stay in the Midwest and head to Indianapolis, Indiana, a city known for its love of basketball.

After the Fever selected Clark, the Los Angeles Sparks selected Cameron Brink, the Stanford University center celebrated for her defensive abilities. Next, the Chicago Sky selected Kamilla Cardoso, the South Carolina center who had played a big role in the Gamecocks' championship win against the Hawkeyes in the NCAA Tournament. Angel Reese also went to the Sky as the seventh overall pick.

NEW CITY, NEW TEAMMATES

Clark moved to Indianapolis to start her journey with the Fever. She had to quickly adapt to a new routine. Clark had graduated from the University of Iowa with a major in marketing and a minor in communication studies, earning a spot on the Academic All-America Team.

Due to the WNBA training schedule, Clark missed her college graduation ceremony. Her new Fever teammates helped her celebrate the milestone with a ceremony at training camp. They even presented her with an unofficial certificate of graduation.

Clark's fame soon became evident to her Fever teammates. During a preseason trip to play the Dallas Wings, fans chased the team through the airport seeking autographs from Clark. A crowd gathered outside their bus before their season debut against the Connecticut Sun to catch a glimpse of her.

HOW THE DRAFT WORKS

The WNBA Draft consists of three rounds with 12 picks each. The order of picks is determined by the teams' performances in the previous regular season, with the lowest-ranking teams going first and the champion going last. However, the first four picks of the first round are decided by a draft lottery. In 2024, the Fever won the draft lottery. Since Clark was expected to be the number one pick, she knew she had an excellent chance of being drafted by a Midwest team close to her home state of Iowa.

As the team adjusted to Clark's celebrity, she faced high expectations and had to find her place as she adjusted to playing with new teammates. "You don't want to say too much, you don't want to say too little . . . and so it was hard," she said.[5] Her first game with the Fever was on May 14, 2024, just a month after her college season ended.

DEBUT GAME WITH THE FEVER

A sold-out crowd attended Clark's debut with the Fever, with fans lining up more than two hours before the game began. Clark's debut as a professional didn't go as she hoped. Although she scored 20 points, she also committed ten turnovers, and Indiana lost to the

PAY INEQUALITY

As a rookie in the WNBA, Clark's starting salary was $76,535. The NBA's 2024 number one draft pick, Zaccharie Risacher, earned $12.6 million as a rookie.[6] This pay gap highlights the long-standing challenge of gender inequality in professional sports. The NBA sells broadcasting rights at higher prices, has more ticket and merchandise sales, and receives greater media attention. WNBA players seeking more equity aren't asking to be paid the same as players in the NBA. Instead, these players are asking to be paid the same percentage of revenue that NBA players receive when their jerseys are sold.

In her debut game against the Sun, Clark scored five of her attempted 15 field goals and four of her attempted 11 three-pointers.

Sun 92–71. Clark was disappointed. It was clear to her and her coaches that she had a lot to learn about the WNBA.

The game was more physical than she was used to, and she would need to be faster and more precise with her passes. "She's a rookie," Fever coach Christie Sides said. "This is the best league in the world. We've got to teach her. . . . And we've got to eliminate some of that pressure for her, and that's on me."[7]

As the season progressed, Clark and the team faced challenges. They struggled to work together, losing their first five games. Clark observed, "There was zero flow within the team. . . . No one really knew what the other person was doing."[8]

The team had little time to practice between games due to a packed early-season schedule. The Fever played 11 games in the first 20 days of the season. The last WNBA team to have such a busy schedule was the Mystics in 2011.

Clark's rising fame meant that the Fever faced intense scrutiny, and the media closely analyzed the team's losses. Clark sometimes struggled, as WNBA players were faster than those in college. To master the necessary plays for the WNBA, Clark reviewed game video with assistant coach Jessie Miller, who commented, "She wants to learn. She's just this fierce competitor that always wants to win. . . . And she's going to try her best to do whatever it takes."[9]

To help the team bond, Fever coaches organized team-building activities such as an obstacle course and a home run derby. Clark developed a positive relationship with teammate Aliyah Boston, the number one draft pick from 2023. The two players shared a pregame routine

Clark has thanked Boston, *right*, for helping her adjust to playing in the WNBA.

where they affirmed one another before heading onto the court.

This routine was caught on camera on August 18, 2024, before a home game versus the Seattle Storm, with Clark saying, “You’re going to be amazing because you are amazing.” Boston responded, “Thank you, you too!”[10] By June, Clark seemed to be more comfortable on the professional court, and she began to score more of her trademark three-point shots. As the team came together, the Fever started winning more games.

CHAPTER EIGHT

ROOKIE SEASON

As Clark's rookie season continued, she began to showcase the skills that had made her famous, scoring more three-point shots, showing her exceptional knowledge of the game, and proving she can be in the right place at the right time to get the ball. The Fever, working better together, won seven games in June. Clark struggled with the pace of play at first, but as the season progressed, she felt increasingly able to score.

At the same time, Clark was still discovering how playing in the professional league was different, and her competitive nature and unapologetic style of play sparked public debates and controversy. Other players

In a 92–75 win against the Seattle Storm, Clark scored nine field goals. >>

Clark and Reese faced off in their first WNBA game against each other on June 1, 2024.

aggressively fouled her, to the extent that the Indiana Fever coaches began collecting video footage of these fouls to submit to the league for review. They believed the fouls were becoming excessive and targeted.

Off the court, Clark, along with other popular rookies such as Angel Reese and Cameron Brink, brought star power to the WNBA and attracted more fans to women's basketball. Television viewership of the WNBA surged by 170 percent from a year earlier, merchandise sales increased, and Clark's jersey became the top seller in the league.[1] Arenas were sold out, and games were moved to larger venues when the Fever came to town to meet the growing demand. Fans lined up for Clark's autograph at games.

2024 OLYMPIC TEAM

Although initially included on the training roster, Clark was not selected for the US women's basketball team for the 2024 Paris Olympics. While disappointed, she understood the decision. The 12 players selected were highly talented, and many had won gold at the 2021 Tokyo Olympics. And Clark hadn't played her best during the Fever's bumpy early season. She set a new goal: making the 2028 Olympic team.

In Indianapolis, the Fever saw a 265 percent increase in attendance at Gainbridge Fieldhouse, their home arena, compared with their previous season. The team's merchandise sales rose by 1,000 percent.[2] When the Fever played Chicago in June, it was the most viewed WNBA game in many years.

RIVALRY WITH REESE

The two most watched games of Clark's rookie season were when the Fever played the Chicago Sky, the team that Reese played for. The media extensively covered these games, promoting the supposed rivalry between the two superstar players. This drew even more attention to the WNBA.

During the first matchup between the two teams, the Sky's Chennedy Carter fouled Clark hard during the third quarter. Reese appeared to applaud the act from the sidelines. The media dissected this moment, reigniting talk of a feud between Clark and Reese. The Fever went on to win the game by only one point, 71–70. Carter's foul, originally termed a personal foul, was upgraded to a more serious Flagrant 1 after the game.

About two weeks later, the Fever and the Sky were back on the court once again. As in their previous game, the teams were evenly matched, with nine lead changes occurring by the end of the third quarter. In the fourth quarter, though, the Fever held on to the lead and achieved a 91–83 victory.

In July 2024, Clark and Reese played as teammates in the WNBA All-Star game, marking the first time they had done so. Clark was enthusiastic to play with Reese and was excited that there were two

WORKOUT ROUTINE

Clark's typical summer workout during her college years included fundamentals, such as making 100 three-point shots and taking 300 total shots. She also did cardiovascular exercises and ballhandling drills, such as switching the ball from hand to hand behind her back. As a WNBA player, Clark continued intense handling and shooting drills, and she focused on gaining muscle and strength to enhance her performance.

rookies on the All-Star team. From her perspective, the rivalry was constructed by the media. She said, "For us, it's just a game of basketball." Reese agreed: "When we go out and play super hard, compete every single day, it's not personal."[3]

Rivalries among talented players have historically generated interest in sports. These rivalries typically focus on players in similar positions. However, Clark and Reese play different positions, and so the rivalry has largely been centered not on their skills but on their identities as a white player and a Black player.

Clark is often portrayed more positively. Even when she taunts other players, she is viewed as passionate, whereas Reese has received negative and racist messages on social media. Although Clark has defended Reese, many of the derogatory and racist comments have come from people who say they're fans of Clark.

Reese was not the only player targeted by racist comments that invoked Clark's name. Some members of the Fever fan base took to social media, using hateful, racist, and anti-LGBTQ language in posts supposedly defending Clark. After a win against the Fever, Connecticut Sun star Alyssa Thomas remarked, "In my 11-year career, I've never experienced the racial comments [like those] from the Indiana Fever fan base. It's unacceptable."[4] Thomas wasn't the only WNBA player to speak out. After the Clark–Reese showdown at the NCAA Tournament, Washington Mystics player Natasha Cloud tweeted, "This is where we need our allies. I would love for our white counterparts who play to step up."[5]

> **"Nobody really should be facing any sort of racism, hurtful, disrespectful, hateful comments and threats. Those aren't fans, those are trolls."[7]**
>
> **—Caitlin Clark, 2024**

Clark said, "People should not be using my name to push those agendas. It's disappointing. It's not acceptable. . . . Treating every single woman in this league with the same amount of respect, I think, it's just a basic human thing that everybody should do."[6]

She also noted that she can't control what happens on social media. But many WNBA players said that Clark needed to speak out against people using her name to justify racist comments. Because of her fame, they believed, she should use her platform to speak out.

ROOKIE OF THE YEAR

Clark and the Fever finished the season 20–20, the sixth-best record in the league, and the team made the playoffs for the first time since 2016. On September 22, 2024, Clark and the Indiana Fever played the Sun in Game 1 of their best-of-three playoff series. This game became the most watched WNBA playoff game ever on ESPN platforms.

In the first quarter, the Fever put up a fight against the Sun, ending only three points down at 23–20. The Fever briefly took the lead in the second quarter but weren't able to hold on to it, scoring five fewer points than the Sun for a deficit of eight at halftime. Clark's team wasn't able to take back the lead after that. By the end of the game, Clark had made only two of her 13 attempted three-pointers. The Fever lost 93–69, giving the Sun the lead in the playoff series.

LIFE IN THE SPOTLIGHT

Clark's first season with the Fever meant living under constant public scrutiny. At times this was challenging. There were moments when she did not want to pose for a picture, such as when she was eating a meal at a restaurant. Nevertheless, she is grateful for her fame. She strives to be the same person regardless of whether anyone is watching, to build good relationships, and to treat everyone with respect, as she says this is how she was raised.

In the next game, Clark scored 25 points and made nine assists, becoming the first rookie to achieve such numbers in a playoff game. However, it wasn't enough for a win. The Sun triumphed 87–81. With this loss, the Fever

Reflecting on the Fever's playoff loss to the Sun, Clark's teammate Lexie Hull, *right*, said she considered it a learning experience.

were eliminated in the playoffs. That same week, Clark was named the 2024 Rookie of the Year.

Clark averaged 19.2 points, 5.7 rebounds, and 8.4 assists per game as a rookie.[8] She had entered the league with huge expectations. After a bumpy start, partly attributed to high talent level and a tough travel schedule, she was able to showcase her skills.

In addition to being honored as Rookie of the Year, Clark set numerous other records her first season. She scored the most points by a rookie and had the most assists by a rookie, broke the rookie record for three-pointers, and became the first rookie to earn Player of the Month honors since the award's inception in 2010. Clark tied the WNBA record for three-pointers in a single game by a rookie when she made seven against the Mystics. However, Clark also had the highest number of turnovers in a season. After a whirlwind year, with the NCAA season, the NCAA Tournament, and her first professional season happening one after another, Clark looked forward to a break.

Over her first year in the WNBA, Clark had traveled around the country to play at different arenas and had faced a tough schedule. The playoffs had given her and the Fever a glimpse of what they wanted to achieve in the future. She felt motivated to work hard as she entered the offseason.

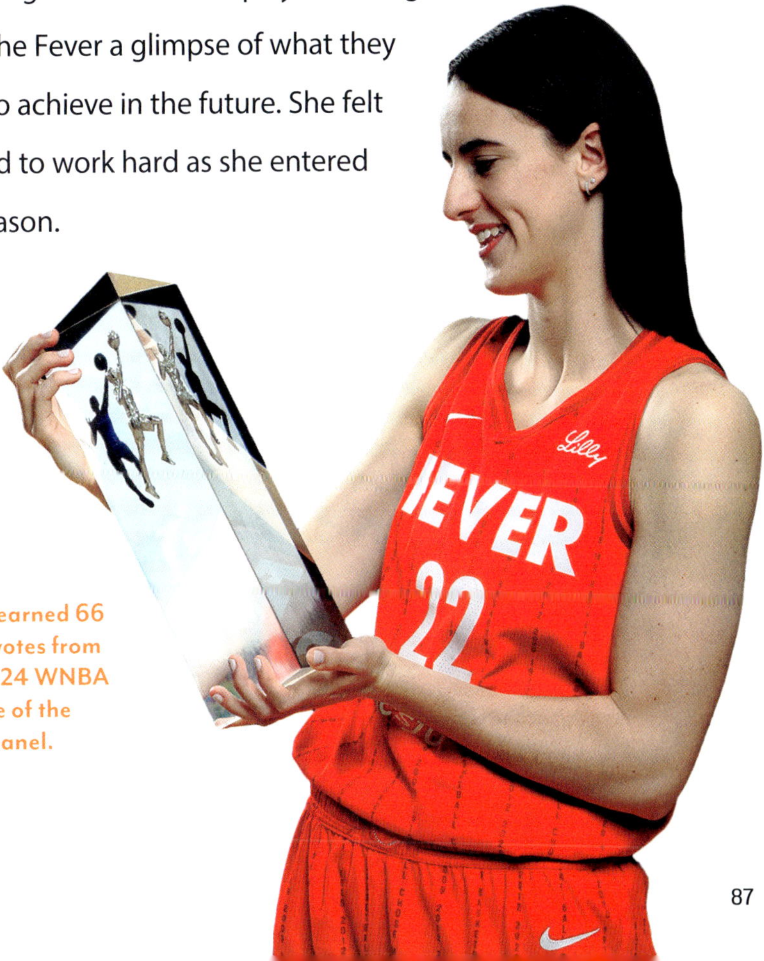

Clark earned 66 of 67 votes from the 2024 WNBA Rookie of the Year panel.

CHAPTER NINE

ATHLETE OF THE YEAR

During Clark's rookie season, she set multiple records, filled arenas, and attracted more attention to women's sports overall. She received many accolades. This included being named the 2024 *Time* Athlete of the Year and the Associated Press Athlete of the Year.

Sports Illustrated included both Clark and Reese in its 2024 list of the 50 most influential figures in sports. For her role in driving interest and momentum to women's sports, Clark made the 2024 *Forbes* list of the world's 100 most powerful women. This marked the first time a basketball player has achieved this honor.

Clark often stopped to sign autographs for fans before and after games during her rookie season in the WNBA. >>

Some young fans of Clark brought supportive signs to her collegiate and professional games.

South Carolina Gamecocks coach Dawn Staley stated, "I want to personally thank Caitlin Clark for lifting up our sport."[1] When asked by *Time* magazine to define her year in one word, Clark chose "historic."[2] She said she feels she has captivated new fans, including people who had never watched women's basketball before.

During Clark's first season with the Fever, many young girls became dedicated fans. They wore her jersey, lined up for her autograph, and held up hand-drawn signs showing their support. Many had traveled great distances to see her play. Clark appreciates these fans and takes time to sign autographs.

As a child, Clark looked up to professional women's basketball players. She wanted to follow in their footsteps when she grew up. The impact those athletes had on her was crucial in motivating her, and she aims to have the same impact on young fans.

Clark's influence on young fans had started long before she joined the Fever. While playing for Iowa, young people came to watch her shoot her famous three-point shots from the logo near midcourt. Clark inspired girls to participate in sports and to imagine their future as athletes. Tickets to see Clark play became popular gifts for young girls wanting to attend games with their friends. For fans who have followed Clark for years, appreciating women's basketball became a normal part of their lives.

GIRLS' RISING PARTICIPATION IN SPORTS

Clark's influence has attracted millions of new fans, a trend that has brought girls out to basketball courts to shoot hoops like Clark. Every year, the Aspen Institute, a nonprofit organization that researches youth participation in sports, publishes a report called *State of Play*. In 2024, one of their top trends in youth sports was the impact of Caitlin Clark. Aspen Institute found that overall sports participation rates for girls had increased during Clark's time at the University of Iowa.

Off the court, Clark has worked to uplift young people. In 2023, she established the Caitlin Clark Foundation, which aims to "improve the lives of youth and their communities through education, nutrition, and sports—three pillars Caitlin believes were foundational in her success."[3] The foundation supports community organizations in Iowa. Among its initiatives, it has donated 22,000 new books to children with limited access to reading material, $13,000 worth of sports equipment such as jump ropes and basketballs, and more than 350 backpacks filled with essential school supplies to students in the Des Moines community where Clark grew up.[4]

HOW FEMALE ATHLETES ARE PERCEIVED

Even though Clark has had incredible influence, women's sports still face different perceptions than men's sports. Clark plays competitively, gesturing with exaggerated body language, arguing with referees, and reacting passionately to fouls. While this behavior is commonly

COMMUNITY COURTS

In March 2025, the Caitlin Clark Foundation and the company Musco Lighting announced a partnership that would place four new community courts at various Des Moines middle schools. Musco Lighting, which sells products including lighting systems for stadiums and arenas, would provide four of its Mini-Pitch Systems, which are courts that can support soccer and basketball. Des Moines Public Schools superintendent Dr. Ian Roberts said, "We are grateful for Musco's partnership, and to now have the Caitlin Clark Foundation join us, in helping us realize this goal of creating more opportunities for our students."[5]

Clark often showed her passion for basketball on the court during her first season in the WNBA.

seen in men's sports, female athletes often receive harsher criticism for similar actions. Male athletes are portrayed as confident or competitive, while female athletes are often labeled as overdramatic or angry. In addition, women in sports are sometimes discussed in terms of their appearance instead of their athletic skills.

Alongside other visibly competitive players such as Reese, Clark is challenging these perceptions by demonstrating her strength, speed, agility, and basketball knowledge. By doing so, Clark and other women are paving the way for future female athletes to be strong, competitive, and fierce without the shadow

> **"People are invested in the game . . . and that's what makes it so fun for me. These people aren't supporting women's sports to check a box. It's going to be the new normal."[8]**
>
> **—Caitlin Clark, 2024**

of stereotypes. Clark said to encourage her young fans, "You should be passionate. You should be competitive. You should be feisty."[6]

Clark's style has attracted a significant fan base interested in her personally. This type of interest in individual players is common in men's sports, and it may help to sustain interest in women's basketball as well. As Clark showcases her competitive fire, more and more fans are tuning in to see what will happen when she plays other talented players, and the more that happens, the more people will remain interested in women's basketball and women's sports in general.

CONTINUING CLARKONOMICS

Clark and other notable WNBA rookies, including Reese, made a significant financial impact on women's basketball by bringing millions of new television fans to the sport. With more interest came more media deals for the WNBA, including an 11-year, $2.2 billion media rights deal with Disney, Amazon Prime, and NBC.[7]

A media rights deal occurs when a sports league such as the WNBA makes an agreement with a specific broadcasting company, such as a television network or a streaming service. The deal gives the broadcaster exclusive rights to show and make money from the league's games and other events. A larger media rights deal generates more revenue for teams, potentially leading to better-paying contracts for players.

Clark has also brought financial benefits to the city of Indianapolis by selling out games and attracting people to local businesses. Cities such as Atlanta, Georgia; Las Vegas, Nevada; and Seattle, Washington, have also seen financial benefits from relocating games to larger venues when the Fever came to play. Despite the significant attention that Clark and other WNBA stars have brought to women's

INVITATION TO THE NBA THREE-POINT CONTEST

In January 2025, Clark was invited to participate in the NBA All-Star three-point contest. In 2024, WNBA All-Star Sabrina Ionescu faced Steph Curry in such a contest, which Curry won 29–26. For 2025, the NBA wanted a two-on-two showdown with Clark and Ionescu competing against Curry and Klay Thompson. However, Clark declined the invitation, stating that she first wanted to compete in a WNBA All-Star three-point contest.

basketball, there is still a considerable distance to cover in achieving equality with men's sports, especially in terms of media coverage and sponsorship funding.

LIFE AS A CELEBRITY

Clark's fame brought both advantages and challenges. Endorsement deals from major brands such as Nike and Wilson made her a millionaire. The Iowa State Fair honored her with a life-size sculpture made entirely of butter. She started the Caitlin Clark Foundation, donating money to help others. First Lady Jill Biden and world-renowned tennis star Billie Jean King attended her 2023 NCAA Tournament championship game, and actor Jason Sudeikis also watched an Iowa game alongside WNBA star Sue Bird.

Clark, a devoted Taylor Swift fan, was invited to two shows in Indianapolis that were part of Swift's Eras Tour. Clark sat in a private suite and met Swift's mother and pro football player Travis Kelce, Swift's boyfriend. Swift has indicated interest in attending a Fever game. At the concerts, Clark, thinking they would focus on Swift, was surprised to see fans taking photos of her.

However, fame and the risks that come with being a public figure meant that Clark required an advance

On January 18, 2025, Clark joined Taylor Swift in watching Travis Kelce's Kansas City Chiefs play the Houston Texans.

security team as well as constant accompaniment by a security guard. In January 2024, after Ohio State beat Iowa in Columbus, Ohio, Clark was knocked to the ground by a fan who stormed onto the court. She had the wind knocked out of her and was quickly helped up and off the court by her teammates and security.

Now, her advance security team goes to locations before Clark arrives in order to analyze any potential threats or risks that might compromise her safety, such

During the February 2 ceremony, Clark's jersey number was retired. This means that no other player for the Iowa women's basketball team will ever wear the number 22 again.

as aggressive fans or large crowds. The security team determines routes for her to travel in and out of buildings with the least amount of risk. When Clark attended the Eras Tour, her advance security team provided her with a 30-page document with instructions on how to move safely through the concert venue.

Clark has come a long way from the empty stadiums of her freshman year at Iowa. Today, Clark is recognized in public spaces, whether at the grocery store or out with friends. She acknowledged that this is not always easy. Clark has worked hard to remain focused on basketball, and she keeps in mind the people that matter most to her: her family, friends, teammates, and coaches.

On February 2, 2025, Clark returned to Iowa City for a ceremony at Carver–Hawkeye Arena to retire her number 22 jersey. In front of a sold-old crowd, Clark watched Iowa beat the University of Southern California. Then she watched as her jersey was lifted to the rafters. The audience included Clark's former Hawkeye teammates and Bluder, the Iowa coach who had essentially recruited Clark since she was in middle school, along with celebrities such as comedian and TV host David Letterman.

Surrounded by thousands of fans, Clark said she was "pretty overwhelmed right now." She specifically recognized Bluder and also mentioned her former teammates, her family, and the behind-the-scenes support staff who "have given so much of yourselves to allow me to be who I am. Thank you. I can't say it enough."[9]

ESSENTIAL FACTS

Full Name: Caitlin Elizabeth Clark

Date of Birth: January 22, 2002

Place of Birth: Des Moines, Iowa

Parents: Brent Clark and Anne Nizzi-Clark

Education: Dowling Catholic High School, University of Iowa

RISE TO STARDOM

- Caitlin Clark's outstanding athletic talent caught the attention of college recruiters early on.
- Clark went on to attend the University of Iowa, where her talent in sinking three-point shots became well-known.
- Her exceptional skills and competitive spirit put her in the spotlight, leading to a surge in popularity for women's college basketball.

CAREER HIGHLIGHTS

- In March 2023, Clark and the Iowa Hawkeyes advanced to the championship game of the NCAA Tournament.
- In March 2024, Clark became the highest scorer in the history of Division I college basketball, surpassing Pete Maravich's record of 3,667 points, which was set in 1970.

- Clark was drafted first in the WNBA draft by the Indiana Fever and went on to become the 2024 WNBA Rookie of the Year. She also earned numerous other accolades, including being recognized as the 2024 *Time* Athlete of the Year.

TEAMS

- Dowling Catholic High School Maroons (2016–2020)
- Team USA Under-16 (2017)
- Team USA Under-19 (2019)
- University of Iowa Hawkeyes (2020–2024)
- Team USA Under-19 (2021)
- Indiana Fever (2024–)

QUOTE

"As a young girl I was super competitive. . . . Any sport I was doing, but especially in basketball, I always wanted to be the best, and there [were] times where I definitely wasn't. . . . You get back up and you keep trying."

—Caitlin Clark, March 2024

GLOSSARY

accolade

An award, approval, praise, or privilege granted as an acknowledgment of merit.

altitude

Height above sea level.

athleticism

The combination of physical qualities, such as speed, strength, and agility, that allow an athlete to excel.

body language

Nonverbal communication through gestures and movements such as posture and facial expressions.

burnout

A state in which a person loses interest in an activity due to physical or mental exhaustion.

commissioner

The head of a professional sports league.

double standard

Rules or principles that are unfairly applied in different ways to different people or groups.

draft

An event in which professional sports teams gain exclusive rights to new players.

endorsement

A form of advertising in which a person, usually a celebrity, publicly declares support for a product or service.

perseverance
Continued effort to achieve something difficult despite obstacles or delay.

phenomenon
A notable person or event.

prodigy
A young person who shows qualities or abilities that are exceptionally advanced for their age.

racist
Having discriminatory or hateful attitudes or behaviors against people on the basis of their belonging to a particular racial or ethnic group.

rivalry
A long-term competitive relationship between two or more athletes or teams.

scrutiny
A detailed and critical observation or examination of something or someone.

sketch
A short, comical performance or scene.

stereotype
An oversimplified or unfair idea about a particular group of people.

triple-double
A feat in which a basketball player records at least 10 points, 10 assists, and 10 rebounds in a single game.

ADDITIONAL RESOURCES

SELECTED BIBLIOGRAPHY

Gregory, Sean. "2024 Athlete of the Year: Caitlin Clark." *Time*, 10 Dec. 2024, time.com. Accessed 14 Apr. 2025.

McGrath, Maggie. "Why Caitlin Clark Is One of the World's 100 Most Powerful Women in 2024." *Forbes*, 11 Dec. 2024, forbes.com. Accessed 14 Feb. 2025.

Murrey, Ben. "Clarkonomics: The Impact of Caitlin Clark on Iowa's Economy." *Common Sense Institute*, 21 Mar. 2024, commonsenseinstituteus.org. Accessed 10 Feb. 2025.

FURTHER READINGS

Hendricks, Maggie. *Angel Reese*. Abdo, 2026.

Hoehn, Jim. *WNBA*. Abdo, 2021.

Megdal, Howard. *Becoming Caitlin Clark*. Triumph Books, 2025.

ONLINE RESOURCES

To learn more about Caitlin Clark, please visit **abdobooklinks.com** or scan this QR code. These links are routinely monitored and updated to provide the most current information available.

MORE INFORMATION

For more information on this subject, contact or visit the following organizations:

CAITLIN CLARK FOUNDATION

caitlinclarkfoundation.org

The Caitlin Clark Foundation runs numerous campaigns aimed at improving the lives of young people through education, nutrition, and sports.

INDIANA FEVER

125 S. Pennsylvania St.
Indianapolis, IN 46204
fever.wnba.com

The Indiana Fever has been part of the WNBA since 2000. Its website allows fans to buy game tickets and Fever merchandise. Visitors can also read about players and view updated statistics.

NAISMITH MEMORIAL BASKETBALL HALL OF FAME

1000 Hall of Fame Ave.
Springfield, MA 01105
hoophall.com

The Naismith Memorial Basketball Hall of Fame chronicles the legacies of basketball's most significant figures, including Caitlin Clark.

SOURCE NOTES

CHAPTER 1. THE TIPPING POINT

1. Aaron Marner. "LeBron James, Ja Morant among Fans to React to Iowa Basketball Star Caitlin Clark's Big Game vs. Michigan." *Hawk Central*, 28 Feb. 2022, hawkcentral.com. Accessed 5 June 2025.

2. Emma Hruby. "Big Ten Women's Basketball Tournament Sells Out for the First Time Ever." *Just Women's Sports*, 26 Feb. 2024, justwomenssports.com. Accessed 6 June 2025.

3. "Lisa Bluder Postgame Press Conference 2/27/2022." *YouTube*, uploaded by Iowa Hawkeyes, 27 Feb. 2022, youtube.com.

4. "Lisa Bluder Postgame Press Conference."

5. Ben Murrey. "Clarkonomics: The Impact of Caitlin Clark on Iowa's Economy." *Common Sense Institute Iowa*, 21 Mar. 2024, commonsenseinstituteus.org. Accessed 6 June 2025.

6. Phil Helsel and Rebecca Cohen. "Iowa's Caitlin Clark Breaks 'Pistol' Pete Maravich's NCAA Division I Scoring Record." *NBC News*, 3 Mar. 2024, nbcnews.com. Accessed 6 June 2025.

7. Corbin McGuire. "The Caitlin Clark Effect." *NCAA*, 15 Feb. 2024, ncaa.org. Accessed 10 June 2025.

CHAPTER 2. PLAYING SPORTS WITH THE BOYS

1. Sam Gillette. "Caitlin Clark Reveals to David Letterman That She Used to Drive Her Parents Crazy for Doing This (Exclusive)." *People*, 25 Mar. 2025, people.com. Accessed 6 June 2025.

2. Bryan Murphy. "Inside Caitlin Clark's Family Tree." *Sporting News*, 14 May 2024, sportingnews.com. Accessed 6 June 2025.

3. "Caitlin Clark Tells Her Whole Hoops Story—from Childhood to Iowa to the WNBA Draft | Inside Look." *YouTube*, uploaded by ESPN, 22 Mar. 2024, youtube.com.

4. Grace Raynor. "Iowa's Caitlin Clark and the Stories Only Those Who've Known Her Forever Can Tell." *Athletic*, 31 Mar. 2023, nytimes.com. Accessed 6 June 2025.

CHAPTER 3. DEVELOPING SKILLS AND STYLE

1. Chad Leistikow. "Why Iowa Basketball's Caitlin Clark Could Have Been a Superstar in Soccer, Too." *Hawk Central*, 9 Feb. 2024, hawkcentral.com. Accessed 9 June 2025.

2. Walter Villa. "After a Measured Approach to Trials, Recruit Caitlin Clark Riding High with USA Basketball." *ESPN*, 30 May 2017, espn.com. Accessed 9 June 2025.

3. "Dowling Catholic High School Student-Athlete Named Gatorade Iowa Girls Basketball Player of the Year." *Gatorade Player of the Year*, 8 Mar. 2019, playeroftheyear.gatorade.com. Accessed 9 June 2025.

4. Eric Olson. "Caitlin Clark Was a Grade-School Phenom. Her 60-Point Game in High School Was Sign of Things to Come." *Associated Press*, 6 Feb. 2024, apnews.com. Accessed 9 June 2025.

CHAPTER 4. COLLEGE RECRUITMENT

1. Chloe Peterson. "'We Knew That She Was the Special One': Caitlin Clark Dominating in Her First Season with the Iowa Women's Basketball Team." *Daily Iowan*, 23 Mar. 2021, dailyiowan.com. Accessed 9 June 2025.

2. Adam Hensley. "Driven with Confidence: How Caitlin Clark Became a Hawkeye." *Sports Illustrated Iowa Hawkeyes*, 22 Apr. 2020, si.com. Accessed 9 June 2025.

3. Hensley, "Driven with Confidence."

4. Grant Young. "Former Notre Dame Coach Details Caitlin Clark's 'Soft Commitment' before Iowa Switch." *Women's Fastbreak Sports Illustrated*, 15 Jan. 2025, si.com. Accessed 9 June 2025.

CHAPTER 5. NUMBER 22 IOWA

1. Dargan Southard. "Iowa Women's Basketball: Caitlin Clark's Riveting Collegiate Debut Pushes Hawkeyes Past Northern Iowa." *Hawk Central*, 27 Nov. 2020, hawkcentral.com. Accessed 9 June 2025.

2. Emma Hruby. "Iowa Coach Recalls 'Frustrating Moments' in Caitlin Clark's First Season." *Just Women's Sports*, 13 Oct. 2023, justwomenssports.com. Accessed 9 June 2025.

3. Chloe Peterson. "'We Knew That She Was the Special One': Caitlin Clark Dominating in Her First Season with the Iowa Women's Basketball Team." *Daily Iowan*, 23 Mar. 2021, dailyiowan.com. Accessed 9 June 2025.

4. Myron Medcalf. "Paige Bueckers, Chet Holmgren and 25 More of College Basketball's Most Marketable Players." *ESPN*, 19 Aug. 2021, espn.com. Accessed 9 June 2025.

5. Chloe Peterson. "Caitlin Clark Increases Iowa Women's Basketball Team's National Presence." *Daily Iowan*, 30 Jan. 2022, dailyiowan.com. Accessed 9 June 2025.

6. Peterson, "Caitlin Clark Increases Iowa Women's Basketball Team's National Presence."

7. Chloe Peterson. "Iowa Women's Basketball Playing with Chip on Shoulder After Early-Round NCAA Tournament Exit in 2022." *Daily Iowan*, 16 Mar. 2023, dailyiowan.com. Accessed 9 June 2025.

8. Dargan Southard. "Caitlin Clark's 10 Biggest Moments En Route to the NCAA Women's Basketball Scoring Record." *Hawk Central*, 15 Feb. 2024, hawkcentral.com. Accessed 9 June 2025.

CHAPTER 6. THE CAITLIN CLARK EFFECT

1. Wright Thompson. "Caitlin Clark and Iowa Find Peace in the Process." *ESPN*, 20 Mar. 2024, espn.com. Accessed 9 June 2025.

2. Patrick Andres. "'When Other People Do It, Y'all Say Nothing': Angel Reese Sounds Off on Critics After Title Game." *Sports Illustrated*, 2 Apr. 2023, si.com. Accessed 9 June 2025.

3. Thompson, "Caitlin Clark and Iowa Find Peace."

SOURCE NOTES

4. Alex Myers. "Iowa Basketball Superstar Caitlin Clark Says Golf (!) Has Helped Her on the Court." *Golf Digest*, 24 Sept. 2023, golfdigest.com. Accessed 6 June 2025.

5. Mike Brehm. "ESPN Gets Record Ratings for Iowa-South Carolina, LSU-Virginia Tech Women's Final Four." *USA Today*, 1 Apr. 2023, usatoday.com. Accessed 11 July 2025.

6. Emma Hruby. "Caitlin Clark Drives Up Ticket Prices for Iowa Basketball." *Just Women's Sports*, 8 Nov. 2023, justwomenssports.com. Accessed 9 June 2025.

7. Courtney Cox and Francesca Paris. "When Caitlin Clark Comes to Town." *New York Times*, 8 Mar. 2024, nytimes.com. Accessed 9 June 2025.

8. Phil Helsel and Rebecca Cohen. "Iowa's Caitlin Clark Breaks 'Pistol' Pete Maravich's NCAA Division I Scoring Record." *NBC News*, 3 Mar. 2024, nbcnews.com. Accessed 9 June 2025.

9. Sean Gregory. "2024 Athlete of the Year: Caitlin Clark." *Time*, 10 Dec. 2024, time.com. Accessed 9 June 2025.

CHAPTER 7. JOINING THE WNBA

1. Sean Neumann. "Caitlin Clark Lands Historic $28 Million Shoes Deal with Nike That Includes Signature Shoe: Reports." *People*, 24 Apr. 2024, people.com. Accessed 9 June 2025.

2. "Caitlin Clark's Pre-WNBA Draft Interview on Transitioning to the Pros & More | WNBA Countdown." *YouTube*, uploaded by ESPN, 15 Apr. 2024, youtube.com.

3. Rachel G. Bowers. "What Caitlin Clark Said after Being Taken No. 1 by Indiana Fever in 2024 WNBA Draft." *USA Today*, 15 Apr. 2024, usatoday.com. Accessed 9 June 2025.

4. "The Historic Arrival of Caitlin Clark | Original Documentary." *YouTube*, uploaded by Trice, 17 Nov. 2024, youtube.com.

5. "Caitlin Clark on 'Life Changing' Rookie Year, Chiefs Fandom, NBA Ratings Debate and More | Ep 117." *YouTube*, uploaded by New Heights, 2 Jan. 2025, youtube.com.

6. Adam Wells. "Zaccharie Risacher Signs $57M Hawks Rookie Contract after Going No. 1 in NBA Draft." *Bleacher Report*, 6 July 2024, bleacherreport.com. Accessed 23 June 2025.

7. Alexa Philippou. "Caitlin Clark Scores 20 in 10-TO Debut as Fever Fall to Sun." *ESPN*, 14 May 2024, espn.com. Accessed 9 June 2025.

8. Sean Gregory. "2024 Athlete of the Year: Caitlin Clark." *Time*, 10 Dec. 2024, time.com. Accessed 9 June 2025.

9. Alexa Philippou. "How Caitlin Clark and the Fever Returned to WNBA Playoffs." *ESPN*, 20 Sept. 2024, espn.com. Accessed 9 June 2025.

10. Philippou, "How Caitlin Clark and the Fever Returned."

CONTINUED. . .

CHAPTER 8. ROOKIE SEASON

1. "The Historic Arrival of Caitlin Clark | Original Documentary." *YouTube*, uploaded by Trice, 17 Nov. 2024, youtube.com.

2. "Fans Are Engaging with the Indiana Fever in Record Numbers." *Indiana Fever*, 14 Aug. 2014, fever.wnba.com. Accessed 11 July 2025.

3. Sydney Wingfield and Jacqueline Tempera. "Angel Reese and Caitlin Clark's Relationship: All about Their On-Court History, Rivalry, and Teamwork." *Women's Health*, 19 July 2024, womenshealthmag.com. Accessed 9 June 2025.

4. Scott Horner. "Alyssa Thomas Calls Out 'Racist' Comments from Some Fever Fans: 'There's No Place for It.'" *IndyStar*, 25 Sept. 2024, indystar.com. Accessed 9 June 2025.

5. Mike Freeman. "Reaction to Angel Reese Taunting Caitlin Clark Shows the Double Standard for Black Athletes." *USA Today*, 3 Apr. 2023, usatoday.com. Accessed 9 June 2025.

6. "Caitlin Clark Speaks Out against Racist, Misogynistic Comments." *ESPN*, 14 June 2024, espn.com. Accessed 9 June 2025.

7. Matthew Glenesk. "Caitlin Clark: 'Those Aren't Fans, Those Are Trolls.' Fever Star on Racist Online Abuse." *IndyStar*, 27 Sept. 2024, indystar.com. Accessed 9 June 2025.

8. Jack Maloney. "Caitlin Clark's Historic Rookie Season, Contextualized: Where Fever Star's Debut Campaign Ranks All-Time." *CBS Sports*, 20 Sept. 2024, cbssports.com. Accessed 9 June 2025.

CHAPTER 9. ATHLETE OF THE YEAR

1. Doug Feinberg. "Caitlin Clark Honored as AP Female Athlete of the Year following Her Impact on Women's Sports." *Associated Press*, 24 Dec. 2024, apnews.com. Accessed 9 June 2025.

2. Sean Gregory. "2024 Athlete of the Year: Caitlin Clark." *Time*, 10 Dec. 2024, time.com. Accessed 9 June 2025.

3. "Caitlin Clark Foundation." *Caitlin Clark Foundation*, n.d. caitlinclarkfoundation.org. Accessed 10 June 2025.

4. "The Caitlin Clark Foundation Hosts Back-to-School Backpacks Event." *Caitlin Clark Foundation*, 2 Aug. 2024, caitlinclarkfoundation.org. Accessed 9 June 2025.

5. "Caitlin Clark Foundation Community Courts." *Caitlin Clark Foundation*, 18 Mar. 2025, caitlinclarkfoundation.org. Accessed 9 June 2025.

6. "Iowa Everywhere Exclusive. Getting to Know Caitlin Clark." *YouTube*, uploaded by Iowa Everywhere, 20 Feb. 2023, youtube.com.

7. Maggie McGrath. "Why Caitlin Clark Is One of the World's 100 Most Powerful Women in 2024." *Forbes*, 11 Dec. 2024, forbes.com. Accessed 9 June 2025.

8. Gregory, "2024 Athlete of the Year."

9. Office of Strategic Communication. "From the Logo to the Rafters: Iowa Retires Caitlin Clark's Jersey." *Iowa Now*, 3 Feb. 2025, now.uiowa.edu. Accessed 9 June 2025.

INDEX

ABOUT THE AUTHOR

MEGAN CLENDENAN

Megan Clendenan is a children's book author and freelance writer. She loves reading and writing books about adventure, history, fascinating people, and the environment. She lives near Vancouver, British Columbia, with her family and two fuzzy orange cats.